Jams and Jellies

HOW THEY USED TO DO IT

Copyright © 2013 Two Magpies Publishing

An imprint of Read Publishing Ltd
Home Farm, 44 Evesham Road,
Cookhill, Alcester,
Warwickshire, B49 5LJ

Commissioning Editor Rose Hewlett
Written by Amelia Carruthers
Design by Zoë Horn Haywood

All Images remain the copyright property of their respective owners, all attributions and copyright licences are referenced at the rear of the book.

This book is copyright and may not be reproduced or copied in any way without the express permission of the publisher in writing.

British Library Cataloguing-in-Publication Data.
A catalogue record for this book is available from the British Library.

Contents

Introduction 3

Jams and Jellies:
  A History..................................9

The Story of the Store Cupboard 13
  Staple Ingredients........................17

Sourcing
Your Supplies...............................27

Equipment and Preparation 31
  Equipment Checklist 36

Measurements................................37

Essential Skills............................43

Recipes 49
  Crab Apple Jelly 52
  Elderflower Jelly 56
  Quince Jam................................62
  Rhubarb and Rosehip Jam 66
  Blackberry Jam 72
  Strawberry Jam 76
  Raspberry Jelly 80
  Red Currant Jelly 84
  Damson Jelly..............................90
  Lemon Marmalade 94

Contents

Orange Marmalade 99
Plum Jam 102
Apricock Confiture 106
Gooseberry Jam 112
Lavender Jelly 116
Rose Jam 120
Rose Petals 124
Dandelion Jelly 126
Spiced Blueberry Jam 132
Cranberry Jam 136
Pineapple Jam 140
Ginger Jelly 144
Winter Spiced Jelly 148
Apple and Mint Jelly .154
Basil Jelly 158
Sage and Tarragon Jelly 162
Wild Rowan Jam 166
English Herb Jelly 170

Serving
Suggestions 175
  Brave enough for these? 178

Gorgeous Gifts 181

'SOME BOOKS ARE TO BE TASTED, OTHERS TO BE SWALLOWED, AND SOME FEW TO BE CHEWED AND DIGESTED.'

Francis Bacon

Foreword

The simple pleasure of mastering practical household skills has been all but forgotten over the last century. We live in an overly convenient, disposable world in which things arrive pre-packed, ready-wrapped and lacking in any craft, care, or quality.

It's time to reject this attrition of what were once everyday skills, time to get back to basics, time to remember How They Used To Do It! The 'How They Used To Do It' series will take you back to the golden age of practical skills; an age where making and mending, cooking and preserving, brewing and bottling, were all done within the home. This fun, and proudly *kitsch* series will instruct you in a whole range of traditional skills that have fallen out of use, putting old knowledge into new hands. Using household items, nifty hints and tricks, and a little creativity you will be surprised what you can achieve.

The series has been carefully curated from a wealth of original resources to provide a wonderful blend of social history and practical instruction. The knowledge within these pages has been sourced from rare books, old newspapers and forgotten magazines to inform a whole new generation about *How They Used To Do It*.

Introduction

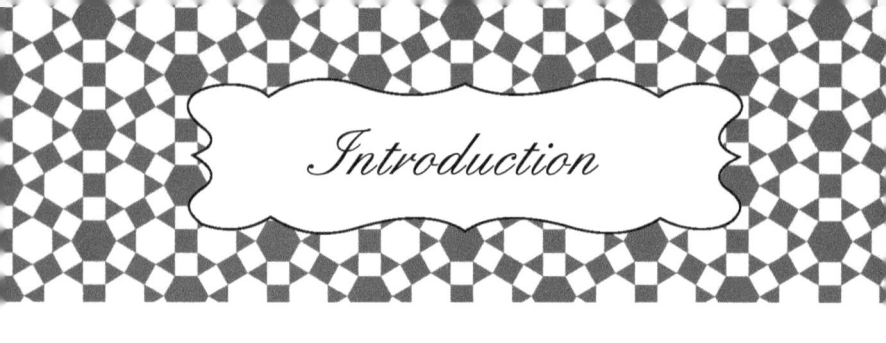

Introduction

WELCOME TO THE WONDERFUL WORLD OF JAMS AND JELLIES.

Introduction

The main benefit of homemade jellies and jams is that *you* can pick the best and purest ingredients yourself. In an increasingly synthetic age, knowing exactly what has gone into your lovingly created products is a rare luxury. With just a little time, effort and outlay, the end result is incredibly rewarding!

Herein lies the philosophy behind the 'How They Used To Do It' series. With this little book in your hands you can turn a humble kitchen into a hub of activity, happily passing many a rainy (or sunny!) day creating delicious and refreshing concoctions. As well as lots of classic recipes, this book is filled with tips and techniques on making the perfect preserve. What's more, you don't even need lots of equipment or a vast array of ingredients to get started.

Introduction

Making your own jams and jellies at home is very often cheaper than buying them - perfect for the thrifty home-chef. The cost of ingredients is low (especially if you pick them yourself), and by creating large batches, you can save a huge amount of money. It is *incredibly easy* to make jams and jellies at home… Preserving fruit by turning it into jam, for example, involves boiling (to reduce the fruit's

Introduction

moisture content and to kill bacteria, yeasts, etc.), sugaring (to prevent their re-growth) and sealing within an airtight jar (to prevent recontamination). Thats it! Jellies are largely similar, but generally involve the addition of gelatine and 'straining' to produce a clear end result. The wonderful thing about making your own homemade products is the fun one can have with creating customised labels and garnishes to the finished jars (think berries, citrus zest, herb sprigs) – a perfect vintage-inspired present as well as personal treat. We hope that the reader is inspired by this book to start making their own jams and jellies, a delicious, historical, as well as rewarding pastime. Enjoy.

Amelia Carruthers

Introduction

"Perhaps Ruskin is no longer fashionable, but sometimes I like to remind myself of one thing he wrote concerning cooking. 'Cookery means the knowledge of Medea and of Circe and of Helen and of the Queen of Sheba. It means the knowledge of all herbs and fruits and balms and spices, and all that is healing and sweet in the fields and groves, and savoury in meats. It means carefulness and inventiveness and readiness of appliances. It means the economy of your grandmothers, and the science of the modern chemist; it means much testing and no wasting; it means English thoroughness and French Art and Arabian hospitality; and, in fine, it means that you are to be perfectly and always ladies… loaf givers."

Mollie Stanley Wrench,
The Complete Illustrated Cookery *(1935)*

Jams and Jellies: A History

Jams and Jellies: A History

For time immemorial, fruit has been regarded not merely as an article of food, but also as a luxury. The season during which each ripe fruit could be obtained was in most cases of only short duration, and ripe fruit was exceedingly perishable. Hence, some method of preservation was a matter of importance, and the most convenient (and most generally adopted process) consisted of boiling fruit with sugar - the resultant product being known as preserves or jam! Preservation with the use of either honey or sugar was well known to the earliest cultures, and in ancient Greece, fruits kept in honey were common fare. Quince, mixed with honey, semi-dried and then packed tightly into jars was a particular speciality. This method was taken, and improved upon by the Romans, who *cooked* the quince and honey - producing a solidified texture which kept for much longer.

Jams and Jellies: A History

An old dictionary definition of jam is 'a confectionary preparation of fruit or other vegetable products preserved with sugar.' And one of the earliest references to this means of treating fruit is that of Surflet, who in 1600 stated that 'There is but very seldome any preserves made of the flowers and leaves of herbs; I understand by this preserves taken properly, the presenting of things whole and not stampt and beaten into one bodie.' Here, there is an interesting distinction; between the preservation of whole fruits, and those beaten into one uniform substance. The former are preserves, the latter are jam. The name is said to derive from an old English verb, 'to jamb', meaning to crush or pulp.

Jams and Jellies: A History

These techniques have remained popular into the modern age, especially so during the high-tide of imperialism, when trading between Europe, India and the Orient was at its peak. This fervour for trade had two fold consequences; the need to preserve a variety of goods, and the arrival of sugar cane in Europe. Jellies were a mainstay of the upper-class Victorian table, more used for decoration and display (some moulds were incredibly elaborate - almost pieces of art) than food preservation proper. Made in ceramic moulds, cut jelly shapes were suspended in clear jellies, and multi-part moulds allowed for centres with contrasting colours and flavours. Austerity in the war years soon put a stop to such complex production, but for the common people though, Jellies were most frequently used for savoury items. Some foods such as eels, naturally form a protein gel when cooked - and this dish became especially popular in the East End of London, where they were (and are) eaten with mashed potatoes. Not to worry though, in this *How They Used To Do It*, we'll be sticking strictly to fruits and flowers!

The Story of the Store Cupboard

The Story of the Store Cupboard

"A store-cupboard, from which one can produce pots of homemade preserve, is a great advantage, since with the aid of jams and jellies so many nice dishes can be made. As well as this, there are many delicacies like rowan or elderberry jelly, rose-hip jam, bramble jelly, and many other old-world dainty which can be made from the harvest of the hedgerows, and which it is a pride to be able to set on the table. It is true we do not make so many jams as did our grandmothers, but the processes they used are the same today."

Mollie Stanley Wrench (1935)

The Story of the Store Cupboard

Kitchens have come an awfully long way in the past century, as have the supplies stocked in pantries and larders. Before modern conveniences such as fridges and freezers, one of the biggest hurdles housewives had to overcome was the task of preserving, and it was no mean feat! It is hard to imagine a world without the convenience of modern kitchen appliances, and keeping food fresh was a daily challenge. There are many simple preservation methods that can be carried out in the kitchen, without the use of modern conveniences. Salt can be used to cure meat and fish, and pickling can preserve vegetables. The drying of fruit, herbs and spices is especially useful, and can be used across a wide range of recipes including sweets. Luckily, jams and jellies are also perfect preservation methods!

The Story of the Store Cupboard

Sugar is a natural preservative meaning it could be used by housewives alongside some clever cooking to preserve a glut of seasonal produce or expensive fruits. Having a well-stocked larder was the mark of a good housewife, and before easy preservation and storage methods became commonplace, homemade jams and jellies were *de-rigueur*. Lessening food waste is a thoroughly worthwhile project (both *then* and *now*). During the autumn months especially, when certain fruits are in abundance, making batches of jams to store is a great way of ensuring none of the delicious fruits are wasted. Although the jam and jelly-makers of the past would not have had this option, your homemade goodies can be stored in the fridge (or freezer) for many months, allowing you to enjoy your hard work throughout the winter.

The Story of the Store Cupboard

STAPLE INGREDIENTS

When making jams and Jellies, thankfully - there aren't many. All you will need are: sugar, pectinous or jelly producing bodies, usually some form of citric acid, and the 'main ingredient' for your jam or jelly, whether that is a fruit, flower or herb.

Sugar and Pectin are the two most important, and consistently necessitated ingredients, so it is worthwhile taking a little time getting to know them…

The Story of the Store Cupboard

Sugar

"These high wild hills and rough uneven ways
Draw out our miles and make them wearisome
But yet your fair discourse hath been as sugar
Making the hard way sweet and delectable"

William Shakespeare, Richard II

These days, sugar is a staple ingredient - found in almost all pantries across the country. It is readily available in many different forms; granulated, caster, demerara, muscovado... etc., the list goes on! Go back one hundred, or even fifty years though, and this most certainly would not have been the case.

The Story of the Store Cupboard

The history of sugar is, of course, inextricably linked with the history of slavery - and Britain as a large colonial power had a large part to play in this human exploitation. Before the seventeenth century, in Britain and throughout most of Europe, honey was the main ingredient used to sweeten foods. But after Britain took Jamaica and other parts of the West Indies from Spain in 1655, this changed. By 1750 there were 120 British refining factories, producing 30,000 tonnes of sugar a year from sugar cane. Sugar was heavily taxed though and it was not until 1874 that this levy was removed and sugar became more affordable.

Until the late nineteenth century, sugar came in the form of 'sugarloaf' which was essentially a hard block of the raw material. Housewives would buy their sugar in tall, conical loaves, and trim off what they needed with special iron sugar-

The Story of the Store Cupboard

cutters called sugar nips. If a recipe called for fine, granulated sugar, then a little elbow grease and a pestle and mortar would be enthusiastically employed! Whilst granulated sugar was not far behind, the two World Wars put the brakes on the nation's sugar consumption. It was among the first items to be rationed in 1918, alongside butter, margarine, lard and meat. During the 1930s, the country's love affair with sugar came under attack. As World War II air raid sirens sounded

The Story of the Store Cupboard

throughout Britain's cities, a different war was being fought behind closed doors. Trade routes to the UK were targeted during the war, and food supplies quickly dwindled. On 8th January 1940, bacon, butter and sugar were rationed by the government, followed in subsequent months by meat, tea, jam and much more.

Despite being armed with her government-issued ration book, the average housewife's weekly shopping basket was suddenly much lighter than before. Creating tasty and nutritious meals for the family became a real challenge for many. Sugar became a very precious resource, and a thriving black market quickly sprung up as a result of the strict rationing. With legitimate supplies so very low, mothers had to be increasingly inventive in order to supply their children and husbands with sweet treats. To give you a picture of 'how they used to do it' in the 1940s - The average allowance of sugar was 8 oz (227g) a week.

The Story of the Store Cupboard

Pectin

Jelly production didn't really take off until it was discovered how to extract gelatine from collagen-rich meat and fish stocks. The first written reference to its discovery is in 1682, when a French scientist named Denis Papin recorded his research on the subject. These experiments resulted in a method of removing the glutinous material from animal bones by boiling. People had been aware of this process by the late 1300s however, but it was not until the mid-nineteenth century that jelly-making became common practice.

Now, *How They Used To Do It* differs from the easily available gelatine-sheets we have today, and one of the most common 'jellying' ingredients was pectin found in fruits. As one early chef noted:

The Story of the Store Cupboard

"To make one's own [pectin] is much cheaper and more satisfactory. It is merely a strong solution of either sour apples (rine, pips and all) or slightly unripe red currants, poured into a bag over a large basin and allowed to drip all night. The bag may be squeezed to extract the utmost of this gelatinous material and the remaining pulp put back into the pan with enough water to cover it and stewed again, then the juice added to the first brew."

Clearly, such methods were a cheap and efficient means of jam and jelly making for the home-chef. So experiment at will! If you are less confident 'making it yourself', here is some sound advice from the First World War:

Jammy Judgements: Pectin Replacements

"It has already been mentioned that fruits contain a body known as 'pectin.' The hardness of unripe fruits is largely due to an insoluble substance known as pectose, and during the ripening, this substance is gradually transformed into pectin by the action of natural fruit acids. The amount of pectin in fruits varies considerably, thus apples contain pectin in large quantity, while the proportion in strawberries is very low. As artificial aids to the jellifying of fruit, two foreign substances are occasionally advised…. These are gelatine and agar-agar.

Gelatine
When pure, gelatine is a transparent, brittle substance, having no colour, taste, and smell. It will keep indefinitely in air, and is usually supplied in thin sheets or in the powder

The Story of the Store Cupboard

form… On making a hot water solution containing one percent, or rather over of gelatine, the solution sets to a jelly on cooling, the stiffness of the jelly increasing with the amount of gelatine present…. The setting power of gelatine is materially diminished by prolonged heating, and long-continued boiling will completely destroy this property, as will a much shorter time at higher temperatures of from 230° to 250° Fahrenheit.

Agar-agar
Is obtained from an edible seaweed found in Malacca and other parts of Southern Asia. The active ingredient of this body is gelose, a substance of exceedingly high gelatinous properties. Much higher melting point than that of gelatine."

William C. Jago,
Jam Manufacture: Its Theory and Practice *(1919)*

The Story of the Store Cupboard

For the modern Jam or Jelly maker, 'Agar-Agar' is a great vegetarian substitute for gelatine sometimes also referred to by its Japanese name, 'kanten.' It is widely available from most supermarkets, so do give it a go!

Sourcing Your Supplies

Sourcing Your Supplies

These days, we are incredibly lucky to be sure of a well stocked pantry. Without the convenience of large supermarkets, it could take a busy housewife the best part of the day to fill her shopping basket with supplies for the week from her local high street.

Making your own jams and jellies is a fantastic way to use up surplus produce, much of which you may have grown yourself, or naturally foraged. Work out when fruits are in abundance, what time of year is best to pick them, and most importantly, *where* you can find them. In June, elderflowers are just coming out, whilst in July the blackcurrants make an appearance, followed by plums in September. For the more exotic jam or jelly though, as well as for

Sourcing Your Supplies

necessary ingredients such as lemons, your local foodstore should have everything you need.

Finding the best ingredients before you put your apron on and start cooking is important, as the lovelier your initial ingredients are, the lovelier the end-result will be. Look at the local produce on offer in your area. It is so often the case that the best things to eat are the things that grow locally, are in season, and haven't travelled a huge distance. Not only do these things taste better than their imported counterparts, but it is far kinder to the environment to use what is nearby. Perhaps you have a wonderful local greengrocer who can supply you with seasonal fruit, or a brilliant local health food shop where you can stock up on herbs and spices? Use your local suppliers and their expertise, as their knowledge will be rather useful to you while you are still getting to grips with the basics.

Sourcing Your Supplies

Equipment and Preparation

Equipment and Preparation

Have you heard of any of these contraptions…?

The Gooseberry Snuffing Machine

The Black Currant Stigger

Orange Chipping Machine

No, neither had we! But they are all machines, used in the preparation of jams and jellies in the early twentieth century. Respectively, they were used for topping and tailing gooseberries, removing the stalks from blackcurrants and for peeling oranges. Thankfully though, for small-scale home cooking, you will need very little specialist equipment. The list of utensils and equipment is not huge, but it is important you have the basics at your fingertips. Your kitchen utensils are the tools of your trade, as it were, and you'll get the best

Equipment and Preparation

results from your jam or jelly making if you take the time to source the right tools.

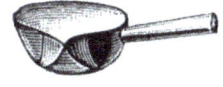

The equipment needed for jam and jelly making is rather basic, and you may already have most of it around the house. You will need saucepans, any earthenware or non-porous bowls and plenty of glass jam jars (for storing both jams and jellies; size and amount dependent on the batch size you are intending), as well as a 'jelly bag' for straining. When you have cooked the ingredients in a saucepan (heavy bottomed jam boilers work best), you may find it useful to purchase a stand or tripod, from which to leave the mixture to strain

Equipment and Preparation

overnight. Though not essential, jelly moulds or decorated glass bowls will add a nice touch. Wooden spoons are great for stirring at high temperatures (as they do not conduct heat), and metal spoons are better for skimming off any scum which rises to the surface.

Always ensure the fruits that you use in your jam or jelly recipes have been washed thoroughly, especially if they have been gathered from low hedgerows, or bushes that are near roads. The recipes in this book will use either 500g or 1kg of fruit (if this is the main ingredient), which should produce between three and six traditional jam jars, or the equivalent of jelly. The amount of jam or jelly you produce will depend

Equipment and Preparation

on how strong you wish the end result to be though. Some people prefer much thicker, viscous jams, whilst others will only be looking for a lightly flavoured jelly. Other ingredients such as lavender, rose or ginger will require much less 'primary ingredient' though, as their natural flavours are so strong. Have fun experimenting and just use what you've got!

Equipment and Preparation

EQUIPMENT CHECKLIST

SAUCEPAN
(preferably heavy-bottomed)

*

BOWLS
(for storing the fruit, or finished jelly)

*

LARGE SPOONS
(wooden are the most useful)

*

SHARP KNIVES
(for chopping the fruit!)

*

JELLY BAG
(for straining)

*

GLASS JARS
(for storage and presentation)

Measurements

Measurements

*"Haste still pays haste, and leisure answers leisure;
Like doth quit like, and Measure still for Measure."*

William Shakespeare, Measure for Measure

Here, we were in a dilemma…

Of course, in the 'golden-age' of home cooking, measurements would have been very rough; using simple ratios was the most common practice. i.e. 'two parts fruit to one part sugar' and so on. Others would have utilised kitchen cups (which, pre-1890s could have been any size!), and yet other jam and jelly makers, as we move into the twentieth century, would have started using ounces, pounds and pints.

Cups have been used in cookery for generations, their use gained in popularity after an American culinary expert

Measurements

called Fanny Farmer introduced them as a standardised form of measurement in recipes. Her emphasis on accuracy and consistency in recipes was groundbreaking for the time, and has since sparked a revolution in the way we cook. Fanny published her best-known cookery book 'The Boston Cooking-School Cook Book' in 1896, in which she stressed the importance of levelling off the cup as you measure. This may seem insignificant, but before her clever intervention, cooks had to make do with instructions such as 'a large dash', 'a goodly pinch', and even 'butter the size of an egg'. Rather amusing, but a little inconsistent, don't you agree?

We are aware that most of our readers will not possess standardised 'chefs cups', and nor may they be au-fait with

Measurements

the exact quantities of a 'goodly pinch.' For this reason, we decided to update all the old recipes into grams; leaving the traditional ingredients and methods - but just making life a little easier for the modern cook.

If you do wish for complete historical accuracy, we have included a handy table for converting grams to ounces to cups, and likewise cups to pints to milliliters. Whether you prefer to don the traditional cup, frilly pinafore and wooden spoon, or take a more updated approach to the classics - we leave the choice up to you…

Measurements

'Cups to Classics' - Conversion Chart

Water	1 Cup	8 Fluid oz	½ Pint	237 ml
Sugar	1 Cup	4.5 oz	n/a	200g
	1 Tablespoon	0.89 oz	n/a	12g

To summarise...

1 cup = 4.5 ounces
1 ounce = 28.34 grams
1 pound = 0.453 kilograms
1 gram = 0.035 ounces
1 kilogram = 2.2 pounds
1 Fluid oz = 29.57 milliliters.

Measurements

More handy weight conversions:

1 Tablespoon = 5 Fluid oz, or 14.79 ml
3 Teaspoons = 1 Tablespoon
4 Tablespoons = ¼ Cup
16 Tablespoons = 1 Cup

Essential Skills

Essential Skills

There really are only two skills the would-be jam or jelly maker will have to master, these are: Sterilisation and Checking the Setting Point. These techniques though, are done in exactly the same way, using exactly the same methods as they always have been. Some things just can't be improved upon!

Sterilisation

It is very important that you use sterilised jars to store your jam or jelly in, both during preparation and in the later stages of the process when you are storing your creations. This will help them to keep for longer, as it will remove any bacteria, yeasts or fungi and protect your liquids. Jars and that have not been sterilised properly will infect the food inside, meaning it will spoil very quickly and need to be thrown away. Sterilisation is a very simple process though, and can

Essential Skills

be done in a number of ways. The simplest way to sterilise your equipment at home is to wash the bottles or jars in very hot soapy water, rinse in more very hot water, and place them into an oven on the lowest setting (275°F/130°C/Gas 1) for twenty minutes. Ensure you use the bottles when they are still warm, and also that they are airtight when sealed to prevent bacteria entering the bottle.

N.B: Do not put cold liquids into hot jars, or hot liquids into cold jars; this may result in the glass shattering; a messy and dangerous problem to fix!

Essential Skills

"The housewife need not be afraid of her preserves spoiling if she follows the few simple directions given here… Complete sterilisation of the glasses and jars, and also the utensils used is necessary if your fruit is to keep perfectly. This is done by immersing the glasses and jars in hot water, or better still, placing them in cold water in a vessel and bringing the water to the boiling point. A little baking soda added to the water will aid in this sterilisation. Keep the glasses and jars filled with boiling water or immersed in boiling water until you are ready to fill them. Don't forget that what is necessary for the jars is also necessary for the lids!"

Mary M. Wright, Preserving and Pickling *(1917)*

Essential Skills

Checking the Setting Point:

Place a small plate or saucer into the fridge (*How They Used To Do It* would have been to cool the plate in water) for roughly fifteen minutes - or until sufficiently cold. Pour a spoonful of the hot jam or jelly on to the plate and return to the fridge for about five minutes. Then, take it out and try pushing the edges of the jam with a spoon or a finger and if it is set, it will wrinkle slightly. Generally, follow the recipes advice on cooking / checking times - however, if your jam or jelly is not set, continue to check every five minutes. It is so important not to overcook - so be vigilant! A slightly 'looser' jam is preferable to one which has a burnt taste.

Traditional Favourites

Every housekeeper knows what a comfort it is to have a good supply of her own preserves which she can rely upon when the winter season comes around, and fresh fruits are hard to obtain or are too expensive.... It is surprising how quickly the pantry shelves may be filled with these delicacies by doing up a small quantity of fruit at a time, and the expense is scarcely felt at all.

Crab Apple Jelly

CRAB APPLE JELLY

Traditional folklore is brimming with references to the apple tree's virtues. This ancient, and thoroughly English tree has provided abundant food for centuries, and has many uses in the kitchen (both sweet and savoury) as well as in herbal remedies. The crab apple (Pyrus Malus) is native to Britain, and is the wild ancestor of all our modern-day cultivated varieties. In 1931, when writing *Modern Herbal*, a Mrs Grieve stated that there used to be 2,000 varieties of apple, but with the unfortunate decline of private orchards, many of these wonderful fruits have been lost.

Crab Apple Jelly

Today though, most wild English varieties of crab apples are red in colour, meaning that your resultant jelly will have a beautiful, pale red sheen - not to mention plenty of flavour! Crab apples are ready for picking in late autumn, so this dish will make a perfect accompaniment to those warming-winter-roasts. Also, try this jelly as a glaze with smoked and cured meats as well as a wonderful addition to traditional gravy, giving a hint of fruit sweetness to your dishes.

Crab Apple Jelly

1 kg Crab Apples
250g Caster Sugar
1 Lemon

Crab Apple Jelly

1. Wash your apples and remove any bruised fruit (leaving this in would adversely affect the quality of the finished jelly). **2.** Place the apples with enough water to cover in a saucepan. **3.** Bring to the boil and cook until the fruit is soft (this should take roughly thirty minutes). **4.** Pour the pulp into a jelly bag (over another saucepan) and let it strain overnight. Remember not to squeeze the bag, or this will make your jelly cloudy. **5.** The next day, add the sugar in the ratio of ten parts juice, to seven of sugar. Also, add a good squeeze of lemon juice. **6.** Bring to the boil, and stir to dissolve the sugar. **7.** Keep at a rolling boil for roughly forty minutes, making sure to skim off any scum which rises to the surface. **8.** Test the setting point (see previous, *Essential Skills*) – if your jelly is set, take it off the heat, if not, carry on cooking. **9.** Pour your jelly into warm, sterilised jars and tightly seal. Voila!

ELDERFLOWER JELLY

"Seven long strides shalt thou take,
And if Long Compton thou canst see
King of England thou shalt be…

As Long Compton thou canst not see
King of England thou shalt not be.
Rise up stick and stand still stone
For King of England thou shalt be none.
Thou and thy men bleak stones shall be,
And I myself an eldern tree…"

Elderflower Jelly

This is the tale of how the Rollright Stones, that lie on the border between Oxfordshire and Warwickshire came to be. When the king and his knights marched towards a town called Long Compton, they came upon a witch (the Elder Mother) who recanted the lines above... The King purposefully strode towards his goal, but on his seventh stride, a hill rose up before Long Compton making him unable to see the town. And thus the King and his knights were turned to stone and the witch turned herself into an elder tree...

The Elder Mother is thought to be the guardian of the elder trees, and it's been said in English folklore that you must ask the Elder Mother's permission before taking any wood from the elder tree, or else ill luck will befall you. So be extra careful when picking her flowers, not to end up like this unfortunate King! Elderflowers are, of course, the

Elderflower Jelly

pretty white flowers of the elder tree. There is a whole host of wonderful folklore surrounding this lovely tree, one such tale recounting that the most auspicious time to encounter faeries is underneath the elder on midsummer night's eve. Its still an important plant today, and one of the main health benefits of elderflowers are that they are antioxidants, cleansing the lymph glands and reducing susceptibility to many chronic (mostly age-related) conditions. Our forebears already knew this; and used elder to protect from rheumatism.

Elderflower Jelly

Elderflowers are best gathered on a warm day (never when wet), just as the many tiny buds are beginning to open. Do remember to leave some flowers for elderberry picking later in the year though. This recipe for elderflower jelly is sweet yet subtly flavoured, and has a gentle, floral aroma. Try adding some sparkling wine into your jelly and garnishing with some of the pretty little flowers themselves, for a truly elegant finish.

Elderflower Jelly

3 Gelatine Leaves
75g Caster Sugar
150ml Elderflower Cordial
350 ml Water
Elderflower heads
(optional, for decoration)

Elderflower Jelly

1. This recipe will be even better with homemade elderflower cordial, but the shop-bought versions will work just as well. It is a really simple cordial to make, though will need about a week to infuse - so prior preparation is key. **2.** Soak the gelatine in cold water (until soft), then drain and squeeze out the excess water. **3.** Place the cordial (homemade or shop bought), water and sugar into a saucepan. **4.** Just before it comes to the boil, remove from the heat and add the gelatine leaves. Stir until dissolved. **5.** Add the fresh flowers if you have them. **6.** Strain the mixture and allow to cool (in a bowl or jars of your choice). **7.** Just as the jelly is beginning to set, try distributing the flowers more evenly. Once cold, your jelly is ready to eat!

QUINCE JAM

"They dined on mince, and slices of quince, Which they ate with a runcible spoon; And hand in hand, on the edge of the sand, They danced by the light of the moon."

Edward Lear, The Owl and the Pussycat *(1871)*

Quince Charming: Quince are small fruits which belong to the same family as pears - and a much under-used and under-appreciated British fruit. Quince trees were first recorded in Britain in 1275, when Edward I planted four at the Tower of London. They may have arrived earlier though, as thirteenth century English recipes included pie-crusts filled with whole quinces coated in honey and sprinkled with ginger (*what a delicious combination*). Gradually though, apples and pears

Quince Jam

edged them out of culinary favour - but now, the Quince is making a come back!

They are grown all over England, and are a treat to find. Pick them in October or November, leaving to ripen in a cool place if necessary. Quince trees are often propagated for their pretty pink flowers, but (we believe) the fruits are best used in jams and preserves - it makes a light jam, perfect for toast or croissants. Quince has an earthy flavour, almost a cross between an apple and a pear, and is also commonly used as an accompaniment to cheese - so why not use it as an accompaniment to the cheese course at your next dinner party?

N.B: Don't throw out the delicious liquid from the first boil. Instead, use the leftovers to make Quince Jelly. In true *How They Used To Do It style,* nothing will go to waste!

Quince Jam

1 kg Quince
500g Granulated Sugar
1 Lemon

Quince Jam

1. Peel the quinces and remove the seeds. Cut them into small pieces and place in a bowl of water (to prevent browning). **2.** Place the quince in a saucepan with just enough water to cover, and boil on a high heat for thirty minutes. They should be nice and soft. **3.** Mash the quince with a fork until the mixture resembles a chunky applesauce. **4.** Transfer back to a large saucepan and add the sugar, lemon and some more water (to get the appropriate 'jam' consistency). Cook for a further twenty minutes, stirring frequently. **5.** Check the setting point (*see Essential Skills)* and if the jam is set, remove from the heat! **6.** Transfer into warm, sterilised jars and seal. Over time the colour of your quince jam may darken – but this is completely natural.

RHUBARB AND ROSEHIP JAM

For something a little different….
…. Why not try, 'Rhubarb and Rosehip' Jam?

"Although this is rather a vegetable than a fruit, and is seldom or never put up as a whole fruit jam by the jam manufacturer, yet there is a fair quantity made in home circles. Forced rhubarb can be obtained in February, and the outdoor growth is fairly plentiful in April and May. For the sake of its pectinous properties, concentrated rhubarb juice has been known as an ingredient of the jams of certain fruits which do not 'jelly' well."

Rhubarb and Rosehip Jam

It is difficult to think of two more traditional English ingredients than Rhubarb and Rosehips. Both have a long tradition of culinary use, and both are also incredibly good for you. Rhubarb is thought to have first arrived in England in the eighteenth century, and was first sold at a London Market by a Mr Joseph Myatt in 1808. Rosehips naturally grow in the British isles and also have antioxidant and anti-inflammatory properties, used as pick-me-ups from colds and flu as well as great for arthritis. These little berries were also used in the Second World War when due to rationing, vitamin C was in short supply. The government actively encouraged groups of villagers to source out these wonderful little flowers in the hedgerows, and share them amongst friends. Share this jam amongst friends, as a wonderful addition to a classic Rhubarb Crumble recipe. It would be fantastic for a summer jelly too, if you have any leftover fruit!

Rhubarb and Rosehip Jam

1kg Rhubarb
150g Rosehips
500g Granulated Sugar
(or more, according how tart your rhubarb is)
1 Lemon
1 Apple

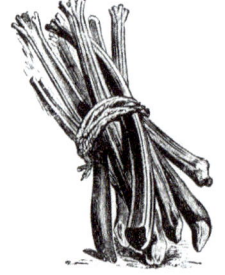

Rhubarb and Rosehip Jam

1. Chop the rhubarb into chunks. **2.** Cut the rosehips in half, scrape out their pips and make sure to remove any straggly or 'hairy' ends. Then, as with the rhubarb, roughly chop into chunks. **3.** Peel the apple, grate the flesh and reserve the core and peel for later. **4.** Combine the rhubarb, rosehips, grated apple, sugar and a squeeze of lemon juice in a saucepan - with water to cover. **5.** Bring the mixture up to the boil and tie the apple peel and core in a piece of muslin, let it cook in the liquid as a source of pectin. **6.** Boil rapidly until soft (probably about twenty minutes), and you can mash the fruit against the side of the saucepan with a spoon. **7.** Test the setting point of the jam – and if it has set, transfer into warm jars and seal. Your English classic is ready for consumption!

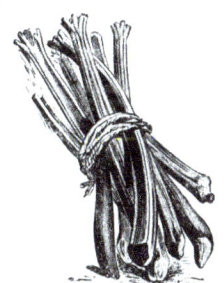

British Berries

Jammy Judgements: Combining Fruits

"The housewife may have quite a variety of delicious preserves by combining different fruits. Inexpensive fruits can often be used with those that cost much more without detracting from the deliciousness of the preserves, and thereby the expense can be reduced. For example… Plums when used alone in preserves are very strong, and many people object to plum preserves on this account. If crabapples are added, the result is a much milder preserve. Rhubarb is usually very cheap, especially in the latter part of the season and can be combined with different fruits to advantage."

Mary M. Wright, Preserving and Pickling *(1917)*

Blackberry Jam

Blackberries are wonderful little fruits, found all over England, most often growing wild in hedgerows. During the autumn months they are in abundance, so why not gather some up to make this delicious jam. It would have been the perfect way to preserve these fruits in times of austerity; easy to find and quick to make… Make sure you rinse the fruit thoroughly before you get started. This will be a delicious accompaniment to a pork roast - especially to give a fruity twist to a rich gravy.

Blackberry Jam

It should be noted that generally, whatever jams you make - these can probably be made into jellies, and vice versa. Jam and Jelly making is a fun, and highly personalised business – so once you've got the basic techniques mastered, get creative!

Blackberry Jam

1kg Blackberries
900g Granulated Sugar
Knob of Butter
Squeeze of Lemon Juice

Blackberry Jam

1. Place the Blackberries into a heavy-bottomed saucepan, adding about 50ml of water and the lemon juice. **2.** Bring to a slow boil, and cook the fruit for roughly fifteen minutes (or until soft). **3.** Add the sugar and stir until completely dissolved. **4.** Raise the heat and cook on a full boil for about ten minutes. **5.** Check the setting point of your jam (see *Essential Skills*) – and if it wrinkles then it is finished cooking. **6.** Remove the jam from the heat and skim off any scum which may have risen to the surface. **7.** After this, stir a knob of butter across the surface, and this will also help to dissolve any remaining scum. **8.** Allow to cool slightly, and pour into warmed, sterilised jars. Seal and Label.

Strawberry Jam

"One must ask the children and birds how cherries and strawberries taste."

Johann Wolfgang von Goethe

"The strawberry jam manufacturing season lasts from about the end of May until the middle of July. The first crops come generally from France, where, as a result of the warmer climate, the fruit ripens earlier than in this countries. Later supplies are obtained from the southern and midland counties... Strawberries are comparatively free from pectin, and therefore, when used alone, do not make so stiff a jam as do many other fruits."

Strawberry Jam

The great thing about jams, is that once you've mastered the basics – you can use any fruit (or combination of fruits you like!). They generally just consist of the fruit, sugar and a squeeze of lemon to help everything combine. So for this strawberry recipe, you can use exactly the same measurements and method as the blackberry jam – just changing the fruit for this, the queen of classic jams. This is a really simple recipe for a sweet and vibrant jam. Scottish strawberries are especially famed for their wonderful taste, the colder climate doing these little fruits wonders. Housewives up and down the country could have planted these juicy fruits as wartime treats for the family; all part of the 'grow-it-yourself trend.' Why don't you have a go at growing them yourself? Strawberries have a lot of natural sweetness, so do adjust the sugar levels according to your own preferences. Spread on toast, or even in little sandwiches, it's a wonderful way to start the day.

Strawberry Jam

1kg Strawberries

900g Granulated Sugar

Knob of Butter

1 Lemon

Strawberry Jam

1. Place the Strawberries (chopped into chunks) into a heavy-bottomed saucepan, adding a squeeze of the lemon juice too. **2.** Bring to a slow boil, and cook the fruit for roughly five minutes (or until soft) **3.** Add the sugar and stir until completely dissolved. **4.** Raise the heat and cook on a full boil for about twenty minutes. **5.** At this point, check the setting point of your jam (see *Essential Skills*) – and if it wrinkles then it is finished cooking. **6.** Remove the jam from the heat and skim off any scum which may have risen to the surface. **7.** After this, stir a knob of butter across the surface, and this will also help to dissolve any remaining scum. **8.** Allow to cool slightly, and pour into warmed, sterilised jars. Seal and Label.

Raspberry Jelly

RASPBERRY JELLY

"Quivering, tempting, fine-flavoured jelly is not in the least difficult to make if one knows just how to go about it. A jelly with a delicate natural flavour is much to be preferred to the strong jelly in which the natural fruit flavour has been destroyed in the making."

The brightly coloured juice that you can gather from ripe, fresh raspberries will make this jelly taste as vibrant as it looks. Just like the strawberries, Scotland is famous for its raspberry growing and in the late fifties raspberries were taken from Scotland to Covent Garden on a steam train known as the 'Raspberry Special.' Now thats *How They Used To Do It* - in style! Try mixing this jelly recipe with a hint

Raspberry Jelly

of elderflower and sparkling wine - a delicious combination which will prove that raspberry jelly if for far more than children's parties!

Raspberry Jelly

1 kg raspberries
1 Lemon
50g Caster Sugar
4 Leaves Gelatine
Elderflower and Sparkling Wine
(optional!)

Raspberry Jelly

1. If you are intending to present your jelly in moulds or jars, hold back some of these little fruits and place them in the containers. This will make a lovely finished presentation. **2.** Place the gelatine leaves in a bowl of water until softened. **3.** Place the raspberries, lemon juice, sugar – and either water (to cover), elderflower cordial or wine, in a saucepan and heat on a low heat – until just simmering. **4.** Take the pan off the heat and add the gelatine leaves (with the water squeezed out). Stir until combined, and add more liquid if required. **5.** Once cool, pour the liquid into your jars or moulds – and decorate with fresh berries, or even elderflowers.

RED CURRANT JELLY

Like Quinces and Crab Apples, Currants are another seasonal fruit which can be found in abundance during Autumn. They are grown all over the british isles, in many varieties - all of them delicious - so do experiment replacing the red currants, with white ones, or even the pink variety. If you find yourself with a glut of these delicious little fruits, why not try this simple recipe for currant jelly? Do add more or less sugar than the recipe states according to taste, as the berries differ quite naturally in their sweetness.

Red Currant Jelly

You may be asking why 'currants' are located in the *How They Used To Do It* 'Berries' section… But currant is actually a specific term which refers to a specific type of berry of the 'Ribes' genus - hence all currants are, by definition, berries. They are also incredibly high in natural pectins, and are thus perfect for old-fashioned jelly making without the addition of shop-bought gelatine. This recipe is a twist on one found in Eliza Acton's *Modern Cookery*, written in 1840.

Red Currant Jelly

1kg Currants
(Red Currants are lovely ones to start with)
750g Granulated Sugar
Water

Red Currant Jelly

1. Place the (washed) currants – stalks and all, with a little splash of water in a heavy-bottomed saucepan. **2.** Bring them slowly to the boil and as soon as the fruit is cooked (which will probably take about ten minutes) – add the sugar. **3.** Bring the mixture up to a rapid boil for about eight minutes, and stir the fruit, pressing against the edges of the saucepan to release the juice. **4.** Let the mixture cool slightly and then pour into a jelly straining bag. Let it drip through naturally if you want a completely clear jelly. **5.** Pour this liquid into warm, sterilised jars – and garnish with some fresh berries for added effect.

Old Fashioned Fruits

Jammy Judgements: Jam or Marmalade??

"There is no very clear understanding as to where jams end and marmalades begin. One authority lays it down that marmalades are made of citrus fruit, another that jams are made of crushed fruits and marmalades from sliced or stripped fruits or small berries. But in the former case what of quince, green tomato and fresh fig marmalade, and in the latter what of currant or pear jam?

It is all very confusing. My own personal definition is that jam is sweet and marmalade is bitter – the kind of thing which does not cloy the palate and can be eaten for breakfast.

There is little difference in the theory of jam and marmalade making except that the thick rinds of orange etc., need previous soaking before cooking."

Ethelind Fearnon,
Jams, Jellies and Preserves – How to Make them *(1956)*

Damson Jelly

Damsons have been in the British Isles for a very long time. One frequently stated theory is that they were first introduced by the Romans (from the city of Damascus), though this is highly debatable! What is for known is that the damson is a subspecies of the plum tree – prized for its rich yet astringent taste, making it perfect for jam-making, and varieties are now found all over Europe. The name 'damson' most commonly *only* refers to forms which are native to Great Britain though. An R. Hogg wrote in *The Fruit Manual* of 1884 'the Damson seems to be a fruit peculiar to England. We do not meet with it abroad, nor is any mention of it made in any of the pomological works or nurseryman's catalogues on the Continent.' As time progressed, a distinction developed

Damson Jelly

between the varieties known as damascenes (more traditional plums) and the (usually smaller) types called 'damsons', to the degree that by 1891 they were the subject of a lawsuit when a Nottinghamshire grocer complained about being supplied one when he had ordered the other! Here is a modern-twist on the traditional damson jam; a damson Jelly, which will be sure to impress any household guests. Happy foraging.

Damson Jelly

1kg Damsons
1 Lemon
Granulated Sugar

Damson Jelly

1. Wash the damsons, and add them to a large, heavy-bottomed sauce pan with the juice of the lemon, and about 250ml water. **2.** Bring this all slowly to the boil, and simmer until the fruit is soft. This should take about thirty minutes – though you can test this by squeezing the damsons against the edge of the pan with a fork. **3.** Pour this mixture into a jelly bag – set over another large saucepan or bowl to catch the juice. Remember not to squeeze the bag if you want a clear jelly. You may have to leave this overnight. **4.** Now, measure the juice, and add one gram of sugar for every millilitre of juice produced. **5.** Put the liquid and the sugar back on the heat and stir until the sugar has dissolved. **6.** Then raise the heat and rapidly boil until the setting point is reached (see *Essential Skills*) **7.** Pour your warm jelly into warm, sterilised jars and seal. Once cool, your damson jelly is ready.

Lemon Marmalade

Oranges and lemons,
Say the bells of St. Clement's.
You owe me five farthings,
Say the bells of St. Martin's.
When will you pay me?
Say the bells of Old Bailey.
When I grow rich,
Say the bells of Shoreditch.

This fascinating ingredient really deserves an entire section itself! Lemons have been used in British domestic kitchens for longer than you may think… The first substantial cultivation of lemons in Europe began in Genoa in the middle of the fifteenth century. The lemon was later introduced to the

Lemon Marmalade

Americas and beyond in 1493 when Christopher Columbus brought them along on his voyages. It has been a revolution to the humble-home cook ever since!

Citrus fruits make wonderful-tasting jellies and marmalades, and this one will have the most gorgeous, vibrant colour thanks to the lemon's natural hue. This recipe for lemon marmalade is a classic recipe to master; slightly easier than the orange variant, because you can use a little more sugar. Once you have a supply of lemon marmalade, you will amazed at how many uses you will find for it. Not only can it be enjoyed as a normal marmalade on toast, but it is a really quick and easy way of adding an extra citrus tang to sweet and savoury dishes, as well as mixed cocktails at home. Its also incredibly handy if you are making a lemon-drizzle cake; perfect added to toppings. This recipe uses the juice and rinds - really making the most of this wonderful fruit.

Lemon Marmalade

1kg (unwaxed) Lemons
2kg Granulated Sugar

Lemon Marmalade

1. Wash the lemons and remove the top stalk. **2.** Place them in a large saucepan with about two litres of water, and bring to the boil. **3.** Simmer the lemons for two hours, or long enough so that the skins are soft (you can test by piercing the lemons with a fork). **4.** Take the lemons out the pan, preserving the liquid, and allow the fruits to cool. **5.** Then, cut the lemons in half and remove the pips and pith – saving them for later, (trying to reserve the juice!) and cut the lemon peel into strips – as thick or as thin as you like for the final marmalade. **6.** Tie the pips and pith in a piece of muslin cloth. **7.** Put all of this; lemon juice, rind and sugar, along with about half the cooking liquid back into the saucepan and boil rapidly for about twenty minutes. **8.** Test the setting point of your marmalade (see essential skills), and cook for longer if this point has not been reached. **9.** When set, allow the mixture to cool slightly, remove the bag of pips, and skim off any scum which has risen to the surface. **10.** Pour it into warm, sterilised jars and seal. Your marmalade is ready.

Orange Marmalade

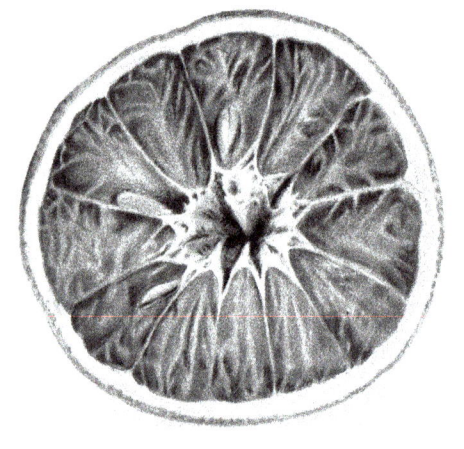

Orange Marmalade

ORANGE MARMALADE

Old-fashioned recipes for orange marmalades tended to utilise 'Bigarade', that is a slightly bitter Seville orange grown throughout the mediterranean region. It had thicker skin and was thus easier to transport on long sea voyages, as well as being high in pectin - perfect for making homemade preserves. These days, the standard 'Seville orange' has replaced this unusual fruit, but it still makes a great ingredient for the home-chef wishing to preserve a glut of seasonal produce. For your perusal, here we have a modern take on the traditional classic. If you are feeling particularly adventurous, try flavouring with dark muscovado sugar and a good dose of Scottish whisky for a truly grown up marmalade. Ginger is also a lovely addition.

Orange Marmalade

1kg Seville Oranges (unwaxed)
1.8 kg Granulated Sugar
The Juice of 1-2 Lemons (according to taste)

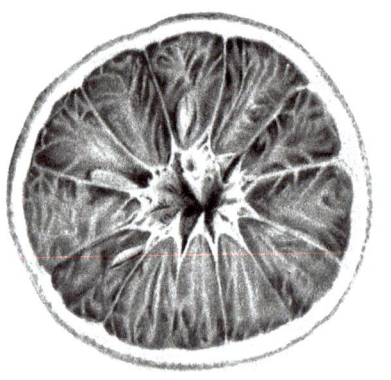

Orange Marmalade

1. Wash the oranges and remove the top stalk. **2.** Place them in a large saucepan with enough water to cover, and bring to the boil. You may need a heavy heat-proof plate to keep them submerged. **3.** Simmer the oranges for two hours, or long enough so that the skins are soft (you can test by piercing them with a fork). **4.** Take the oranges out the pan, preserving the liquid, and allow the fruits to cool. **5.** Then, cut the oranges in half and remove the pips, pulp and pith– saving them for later, (trying to reserve the juice!) and cut the orange peel into strips – as thick or as thin as you like for the final marmalade. **6.** Tie the pips, pith and pulp in a piece of muslin cloth. **7.** Put all of this; orange juice, rind and sugar, along with about half the cooking liquid back into the saucepan and boil rapidly for about twenty minutes. **8.** Test the setting point of your marmalade (see essential skills), and cook for longer if this point has not been reached. **9.** When sufficiently cooked, allow the mixture to cool slightly, remove the bag of pips, and skim off any scum which has risen to the surface. **10.** Pour it into warm, sterilised jars and seal. Your marmalade is ready.

PLUM JAM

"It is as healthy to enjoy sentiment as to enjoy jam."

Gilbert K. Chesterton

Plums are particularly good fruits for jam-making, found in abundance in England during the autumn months. If you are lucky enough to get a glut of these delicious little fruits, making plum jam is the perfect way to preserve the juices of these fruits to enjoy at a later date. Although in most supermarkets you will find mostly foreign plums, this most certainly would not have been 'How They Used To Do it!' Transporting fruit-en masse simply did not take place until relatively recently. British plums are some of the best you

Plum Jam

can get, so picking them yourself is an added bonus. When they are at their ripest, British plums have a tender, satin-like skin, with a delicate white 'bloom' around them, which rubs off when the fruit is handled. The flesh inside is mellow and satisfying.

A perfect ingredient for this little cook-book, plums are gorgeous additions to pies, crumbles, and tarts – as well as a surprisingly good addition to salad dressings. Your jam will give added depth and flavour to all of these dishes – not to mention a pleasant accompaniment to savoury meals such as roast pork. As a final thought... Nectarines are just as wonderful to use, although they will generally have to be shop bought. The *combination* of plum *and* nectarine is a fantastic one too, so why not try replacing half the plums with nectarines, for a truly exciting jam?

Plum Jam

1kg Plums
900g Golden Granulated Sugar
Knob of Butter

Plum Jam

1. Place the Plums (chopped into chunks) into a heavy-bottomed saucepan. **2.** Bring to a slow boil, and cook the fruit for roughly thirty minutes (or until soft) **3.** Add the sugar and stir until completely dissolved. **4.** Raise the heat and cook on a full boil for about ten minutes. **5.** At this point, check the setting point of your jam (see *Essential Skills*) – and if it wrinkles then it is finished cooking. **6.** Remove the jam from the heat and skim off any scum which may have risen to the surface. **7.** After this, stir a knob of butter across the surface, and this will also help to dissolve any remaining scum. **8.** Allow to cool slightly, and pour into warmed, sterilised jars. Seal and Label.

Apricock Confiture

For something a bit different…
… Why not try 'Apricock' Confiture?

Which, as Ethelind Fearnon (1956) somewhat disparagingly states, 'Is simply French for Jam!'

"Take three pounds of sugar, and three quarts of water; let them boil together and skim it well. Then put in six pounds of apricocks, pared and stoned, and let them boil until they are tender; then take them up and when the liquid is cold bottle it up. You may if you please, after you have taken out the apricocks, let the liquid have one boil with a sprig of flowered clary in it; the apricocks make marmalade, and are very good for preserves."

Apricock Confiture

Apricots are a lovely little fruit, a favourite of the Victorian art critic John Ruskin, who described them as 'shining [fruit] in a sweet brightness of golden velvet.' They also used to be called, 'Apricocks'! England is not famed for growing fantastic apricots, however it has happened on a small scale since the sixteenth century – and when they are right and ripe, there's nothing better. Most of our apricots will come from Spain, France, South Africa or California, and they were not widely available (except to a select few English home growers) until the mid-twentieth century. Henry VIII was probably the first home-grower, when his gardener brought back some apricot trees from Italy. Their naturally sweet, syrupy nature will make apricots the perfect addition to your homemade jam repertoire though. Add a bit of honey for some old-fashioned sweet roundness; a wonderful combination.

Apricock Confiture

1kg Apricots
900g Granulated Sugar
Knob of Butter
1 Lemon

Apricock Confiture

1. Place the Apricots (stoned and chopped into chunks) into a heavy-bottomed saucepan, adding a squeeze of the lemon juice too. **2.** Bring to a slow boil, and cook the fruit for roughly ten minutes (or until soft) **3.** Add the sugar and stir until completely dissolved. **4.** Raise the heat and cook on a full boil for a further fifteen minutes. **5.** At this point, check the setting point of your jam *(see Essential Skills)* – and if it wrinkles then it is finished cooking. **6.** Remove the jam from the heat and skim off any scum which may have risen to the surface. **7.** After this, stir a knob of butter across the surface, and this will also help to dissolve any remaining scum. **8.** Allow to cool slightly, and pour into warmed, sterilised jars. Seal and Label.

Flowers and Hedgerows

"JUST LIVING IS NOT ENOUGH... ONE MUST HAVE SUNSHINE, FREEDOM, AND A LITTLE FLOWER."

Hans Christian Andersen.

Gooseberry Jam

GOOSEBERRY JAM

The season for this fruit commences about the beginning of May, and lasts until the middle or third week of June. For jam making, the fruit is used in its unripe or green state, and any sound variety of the fruit may be used without discrimination…. The over ripe fruit makes a 'runny' or pulpy jam, unless very carefully made. Gooseberries make an exceedingly good jam when judged by its physical state, as the fruit is highly pectinous, and thus sets well into a stiff jelly. From these properties, gooseberries are useful as a stiffening agent in other kinds of jam."

This jam recipe used a very similar technique and measurements to the redcurrant jelly already listed. Again, as with most of the fruit in this volume - these gooseberries would be wonderful turned into a jelly, and likewise, the currants could have made a lovely jam. So do feel free to experiment!

Gooseberry Jam

Gooseberry bushes are found all over Britain, in copses and hedgerows and about old ruins - but the gooseberry has been cultivated for so long that it is difficult to distinguish wild bushes from feral ones, or to determine where the gooseberry fits into the native flora of the island. We do know however, that they used to be held in high esteem medicinally for the cooling properties of their acid juices when treating fevers. The old English name, *Fea-Berry*, relating to this usage, still survives in some provincial dialects. Towards the end of the eighteenth century, the gooseberry became a favourite object of British cottage-horticulture. This was especially the case in Lancashire, where the working cotton-spinners raised numerous varieties from seed, their efforts having been chiefly directed to increasing the size of the fruit. Today, gooseberries are prized for their high vitamin-C content, and their tart flavour is perfect in the classic English pudding, a gooseberry fool. Your jam will be a marvellous homemade addition to this dish.

Gooseberry Jam

1kg Gooseberries
1kg Granulated Sugar
1 Lemon

Gooseberry Jam

---

1. Place the gooseberries, the juice of the lemons and about 400ml of water into a large, heavy-bottomed pan. **2.** Bring everything to the boil and simmer for fifteen minutes, or until the fruit is soft and can be squeezed against the side of a pan with a fork. **3.** Then add the sugar and stir until it is completely dissolved over a gentle heat. Be careful not to boil the sugar at this point. **4.** Once the sugar has dissolved, bring the mixture up to the boil for a further ten minutes, constantly stirring and skimming off any scum which rises to the surface. **5.** Your jam should start to turn a light red colour as it cooks – this is a completely natural transformation. **6.** Check to see if the jam has reached *setting point* (see: *Essential Skills*) and if it has finished cooking, allow it to cool slightly. If not, keep the jam on the heat. **7.** Skim off any remaining scum and then pour the jam into warm, sterilised glass jars and seal. Once set, his delicate jam is ready for serving!

Lavender Jelly

LAVENDER JELLY

Lavender is a wonderful flower, famed for its aroma as well as its decorative uses. The English word for lavender is generally thought to derive from the Old French *lavandre*, and ultimately from the Latin *lavare* (to wash) – referring to the use of lavender infusions in baths. Today, you will be extremely lucky to have a lavender infused bath, but use it in your home cooking – and experience the same pleasures. It is a great flower for this *How They Used To Do It* collection, mainly for its many and varied uses. Lavender flowers can be candied and are sometimes used as cake decorations, and it is also grown as a condiment, used in salads and dressing. Lavender also yields abundant nectar, from which our much maligned bees can make high quality honey. This plant

Lavender Jelly

lends a floral and slightly sweet flavour to most dishes, and is therefore perfect when paired with sheep's-milk and goat's-milk cheeses. Try pairing your delicately flavoured jelly with dark chocolate for a truly stunning dessert. Do be careful not to use too much lavender in this jelly though; as it can very quickly become overpowering and overly fragrant.

> *"Lavender is for lovers true,*
> *Which evermore be faine;*
> *Desiring always for to have*
> *Some pleasure for their paine:*
> *And when that they obtained have*
> *The love that they require,*
> *Then have they all their perfect joie,*
> *And quenched is the fire"*

Clement Robinson – Handefull of Pleasant Delites, *1584*

Lavender Jelly

100g Dried Lavender
800ml Water
850g Granulated Sugar
1 Lemon
4 Leaves of Gelatine

Lavender Jelly

1. Bring the water to the boil in a large, heavy-bottomed saucepan. **2.** Remove it from the head and stir in the dried lavender flowers. Let this steep for twenty minutes. **3.** Strain the mixture through a jelly bag into another saucepan. **4.** Add the lemon juice and sugar and stir over a medium heat until the sugar has dissolved. **5.** Then, take it off the heat and add the gelatine (previously soaked in water until soft) – stir until completely dissolved. **6.** Transfer your warm jelly into warm, sterilised jars and seal. Once cool, it is ready to serve!

Rose Jam

ROSE JAM

"What's in a name? That which we call a rose by any other name would smell as sweet."

William Shakespeare.

The quietest of the jams… a perfect jam for those breakfast-time secrets! 'Sub Rosa' literally translates as 'under the rose.' Traditionally, any matters discussed under a rose were to be kept in the strictest confidence, and this is why you will often see roses sculpted into the ceilings of old banqueting halls. What was spoken 'sub rosa', and perhaps more pertinently, under the effects of wine and dining was not to be repeated!

Rose Jam

Roses have a truly heady, delicious scent and in the British summer months, their blooms are everywhere. They are so pretty to look at, but are also great in cooking; used to great extent in Middle Eastern and Indian cuisines. Roses have also been used in English cooking since Tudor times (although they have since fallen out of fashion), but they have such varied uses – to scent honey, make sugared petals for cake decorations, additions to salads, or even… as rose petal jams. Rose jam is delicious served on top of yoghurt, with scones or muffins and as an elegant addition to homemade cakes or biscuits.

Rose Jam

500g of fresh rose petals

500g of caster sugar

1 litre of water

The juice of 2 lemons

Rose Jam

1. Discard any rose petals with discoloration or imperfections – the colour of the rose petals will determine the final colour of your jam, so stick to single variety if you are aiming for a specific colour. **2.** Place your rose petals in a bowl, and sprinkle sugar over them, making sure each petal is covered. **3.** Leave these in the refrigerator for a few hours, for the flavours to infuse. **4.** Place the remained of the sugar, the lemons and the water into a large, heavy-bottomed saucepan and cook on a low heat until all the sugar has dissolved. **5.** Whilst the mixture is not-quite at boiling point, add the rose petals and sugar and keep on a medium heat, stirring constantly. **6.** Let this simmer for about twenty minutes, then bring to a rolling boil for five minutes – or until setting point is reached. **7.** Once the setting point has been reached (see, *Essential Skills*), take the jam off the heat and allow to cool slightly. **8.** Put your warm jam into warm, sterilised glass jars and seal. This beautiful and fragrant jam is ready for consumption.

Rose Petals

ROSE PETALS

If you would like to try making some sugared rose petals (they do make a fantastic garnish to jams and jellies), here is a classic recipe for your own amusement:

"Dip a rose that is neither in the bud, nor over-blowne, in a sirup, consisting of sugar, double refined, and Rose-water boiled to his full height, then open the leaves one by one with a fine smooth bodkin either of bone or wood; and presently if it be a hot sunny day, and whilest the sunne is in some good height, lay them on papers in the sunne, or else dry them with some gentle heat in a close roome, heating the room before you set them in, or in an oven upon papers, in pewter dishes, and then put them up in glasses; and keepe them in dry cupboards

Rose Petals

neere the fire. You may prove this preserving with sugar-candy instead of sugar if you please."

Sir Hugh Platt, Delights for Ladies *(1594)*

Whilst this may sound complicated – all you really need to do is dip your rose petals in egg whites or a simple syrup, and then place them in some caster sugar. No bone bodkins, closed rooms or pewter dishes required!

DANDELION JELLY

For something a little different....
.... Why not try, 'Dandelion Jelly'?

"Are you separated from the object of your love? Carefully pluck one of the feathery heads; charge each of the little feathers composing it with a tender thought; turn towards the spot where the loved one dwells; blow, and the seed-ball will convey your message faithfully. Do you wish to know if that dear one is thinking of you? blow again; and if there be left upon the stalk a single aigrette, it is a proof you are not forgotten. Similarly, the dandelion is consulted as to whether the lover lives east, west, north, or south, and whether he is coming or not."

Alexander F. Chamberlain,
The Child and Childhood in Folk-Thought *(1896)*

Dandelion Jelly

Aside from this lovely folk-belief, today dandelions are thought to be very good for the body, and rather easy to make into a delicious jelly to boot! One of the main benefits of dandelions is that they are purportedly very good for the liver. The antioxidants like vitamin-C and Luteolin can keep the liver functioning in optimal gear and protect it from aging. This is a great as well as highly unusual jelly to make, as Dandelions appear in almost every garden around Britain, allowing for a bit of home-foraging! For a true timeless classic, why not try mixing the dandelion with burdock? This combination has been used in the British isles since the thirteenth century - all the way to the present day. For the first-time Dandelion jelly maker, we have a simple yet classic recipe here:

Dandelion Jelly

500g Fresh Dandelion Petals
500ml Water
800g Sugar
1 Lemon
4 Gelatine Leaves

Dandelion Jelly

1. Collect your fresh dandelion heads and cut off the petals, making sure not to get any of the stalk. **2.** Pour boiling water over the petals and let them steep for about two hours. **3.** Strain through a fine sieve or jelly bag into another bowl. **4.** Add the dandelion infusion, sugar, water and lemon juice into a heavy-bottomed saucepan and keep on a low heat – stirring until the sugar has dissolved. **5.** After the sugar has dissolved, keep the pan on a very low heat and add the gelatine (previously softened in water) and stir until it has completely disappeared. **6.** Skim off any scum which has risen to the surface, test the setting point (see *Essential Skills*) – and if your jelly is ready, take it off the heat. **7.** Allow to cool slightly, and place the warm jelly into warm, sterilised jars. Voila!

Sugar and Spice and All Things Nice

"THE RULE IS, JAM YESTERDAY AND JAM TOMORROW - BUT NEVER JAM TODAY."

Lewis Carroll,
Alice's Adventures in Wonderland *(1865)*

Spiced Blueberry Jam

The juicy blueberry is a family favourite in pies, pancakes, cheesecakes, muffins and fruit salads for centuries. Native to North America, its use has been heavily influenced by American cuisine. The Blueberry was originally utilized by American tribes from the North East of the country, who scoured bogs and forests for this fruit – to feast upon, or to preserve for future use. It was thought to relieve coughs and pain. Today we know that Blueberries are very rich in iron and fibre, but low in sugar. It was used during the Russian civil war as a valuable nutrient drink for the soldiers, and in the rest of mainland Europe, 'Bilberries' (a close relation) were given to World War Two fighter pilots to enhance their

Spiced Blueberry Jam

night vision. The American blueberry was introduced to Britain in the 1930s, and has remained popular ever since. Why not try this winter-warmer as a perfect festive preserve?

Spiced Blueberry Jam

500g Blueberries
450g Granulated Sugar
2 x (10g) packet of Pectin
1 Lemon
75ml wine or Cider Vinegar
¼ teaspoon of ground Star Anise
¼ teaspoon of ground Nutmeg

Spiced Blueberry Jam

1. Place the blueberries in a heavy-bottomed saucepan over a low heat, and sprinkle with the pectin, spices, a good squeeze of lemon juice and vinegar. **2.** Once the berries start to break down, increase the heat and bring to a boil. Quickly turn the temperature down again, and simmer for five minutes – or until the berries are soft and can be squeezed against the edge of the pan. **3.** Add the sugar and enough water to gain a proper 'jam consistency' – and cook until the sugar has completely dissolved. **4.** Once the sugar has dissolved, check the setting point (see *Essential Skills*). Once the setting point has been reached, (probably a further five minutes at least) remove the jam from the heat and allow to cool slightly. **5.** Pour your warm jam into warm, sterilised jars and seal.

"Ripened fruit gleaming red like precious rubies."

This is a lovely festive recipe, which uses the rich, ruby-red fruit; cranberries. Most widely used and grown in North America, cranberries are a fantastic little berry, rich in vitamins C, D, potassium and iron. They are also believed to be a natural remedy for a whole host of health conditions. Cranberries really do come into their own around Christmas, and no hostess's cupboard would be complete without some homemade cranberry jam. They are good for much more than merely accompanying the turkey though, and you can use your jam in both sweet and savoury dishes. As cranberries

Cranberry Jam

can be quite tart and sour, especially when under ripe, do feel free to add more sugar to this jam according to taste.

Cranberries contain a lot of pectin naturally, so this jam should set very well, and make a wonderful accompaniment to all sorts of winter dishes. With this in mind, feel free to experiment with the liquids you use (instead of water), apple juice or cider works well – as would a good helping of port.

Cranberry Jam

1kg Cranberries
600g Sugar
600ml Liquid
1 Lemon (Zest and Juice)
1 Orange (Zest and Juice)
2 teaspoon Cinnamon
1 tablespoon grated Ginger
A pinch of ground Cloves.

Cranberry Jam

1. Place the cranberries, sugar, orange, lemon – and whatever liquid you choose in a large, heavy-bottomed saucepan over a low heat. **2.** Bring the mixture to the boil, and skim off any scum which rises to the surface. **3.** Cook for roughly ten minutes, or until the cranberries are soft enough to squeeze against the edge of the saucepan with a fork. **4.** Add the rest of the spices and continue to stir. **5.** Cook your jam until it starts to thicken – at this point you should check its setting point (see *Essential Skills*). If it has got too thick, feel free to add more water. **6.** If the jam has been cooked for long enough, take it off the heat and allow to cool slightly. **7.** Pour your warm jam into warm, sterilised jars and seal. Your festive treat is ready!

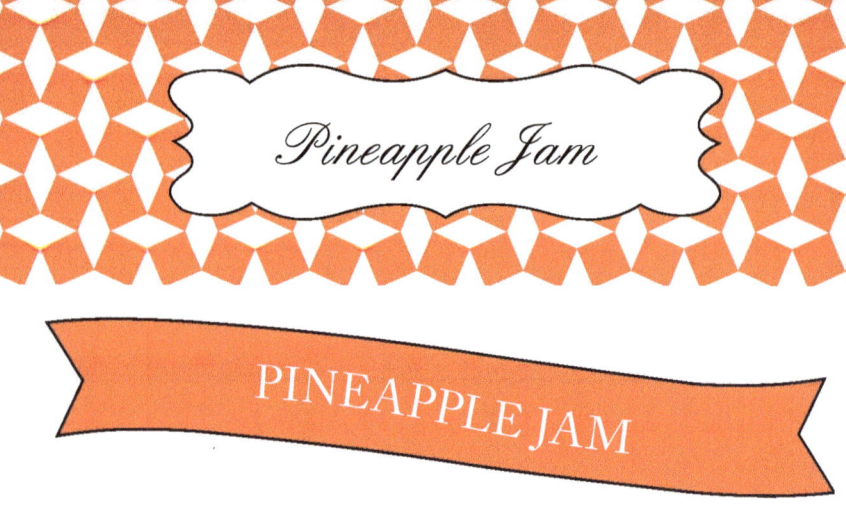

PINEAPPLE JAM

"Variety's the very spice of life, That gives it all its flavour."

William Cowper

Pineapples have been used in English kitchens for longer than you might think! There is infact a painting, created in 1675 by Hendrik Danckerts, which depicts Charles II being presented with the first pineapple grown in England. Whilst this exotic fruit would have been a substantial luxury for the average family, even in the early years of the twentieth century, there are records of pineapple being used. Because of their rarity, finding novel ways to preserve this delicious fruit was even more important! So, in the *How They Used To*

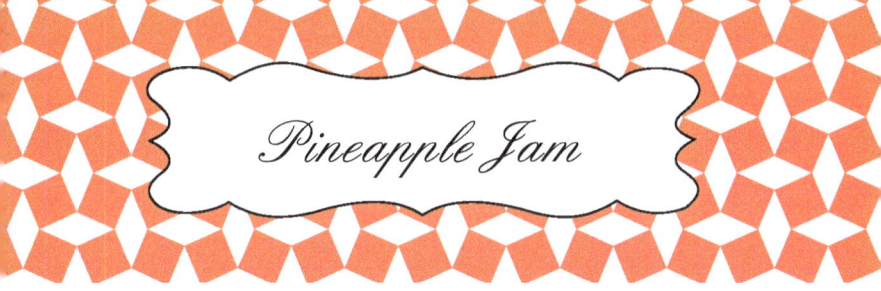

Pineapple Jam

Do It spirit, why not try this delicious spiced pineapple jam? It makes a fantastic and thoroughly unusual spread on toast, as well as a lovely topping for ice creams - and even with a glazed ham.

Pineapple Jam

500g Fresh Pineapple

500g Granulated Sugar

80g Pectin

1 Lemon

1 teaspoon ground Cinnamon

¼ teaspoon of ground Cloves

1 knob of Butter

Pineapple Jam

1. Place the pineapple (chopped), spices and the sugar in a heavy-bottomed saucepan and let it combine for one hour. **2.** After one hour, place the pan over a medium heat and stir constantly until the sugar is completely dissolved. **3.** Bring the heat up to a rolling boil, and cook for five minutes. Make sure to skim off any scum which rises to the surface. **4.** After this, bring it down to a simmer and add the pectin – stirring constantly. **5.** Bring back to a rolling boil for just one minute, then remove the pan from the heat, and again, skim any scum. If you stir a knob of butter across the surface, this will also help dissolving any remaining scum. **6.** Let the jam cool slightly, then pour your warm jam into warm, sterilised jars and seal. Your tropical treat is ready.

Ginger Jelly

GINGER JELLY

The warm and spicy flavour of fresh ginger makes a wonderful jelly, and is a very versatile ingredient to have stocked in your store cupboard. From its origin to the present, ginger is the world's most widely cultivated herb, but sadly, not as appreciated as it should be! Testimonials of both the medicinal and economic importance of ginger have been recorded as far back as five thousand-year-old Greek literature to 200 B.C. Try this simple recipe for ginger jelly, which once made, can be added to an array of desserts and savoury asian dishes to really spice them up. Unlike most of the other recipes, you will not need that much ginger here, as the flavour is naturally very strong. Try with rhubarb for a light and refreshing summertime jelly, or with lemongrass

Ginger Jelly

and lime, as in this recipe - and serve with strawberries or even watermelon. Combined with a little lemon as well, ginger jelly makes a perfect natural pick-me-up for sore throats and colds.

Ginger Jelly

3cm of sliced ginger
300g Caster Sugar
2 bruised lemongrass stalks
2 Limes (juice and zest)
3 Gelatine Leaves
850 ml Water

Ginger Jelly

1. Place the gelatine in a bowl of water, and soak until soft. **2.** Place the lemongrass, ginger and lime zest in a heavy-bottomed saucepan with the water – and bring to the boil. **3.** Once the mixture has boiled, take it off the heat and leave to cool. **4.** Then, strain the liquid through muslin or a jelly bag and return to the heat. **5.** Add the sugar and the gelatine (soft with the excess water squeezed out) and place over a very low heat – stirring constantly until everything is dissolved. Do not allow this to boil – if you do, the setting properties of the gelatine will not work. **6.** Remove from the heat and add the lime juice. **7.** Pour your warm jelly into warm, sterilised jars and seal. Serve with refreshing fruit on a summer's day!

WINTER SPICED JELLY

For something a little different….
…. Why not try, 'Winter Spiced Jelly'?

This spiced winter jelly uses a very traditional array of mulling spices – making it an exceptionally good accompaniment to a festive meat and cheese board. These spices are usually used to flavour drinks such as hot apple cider, mulled wine and wassail during the autumn and winter, but as is evident here, can be used for a whole array of purposes. The traditional definition of 'mulled' is a drink which has been prepared with these spices – usually through heating the drink in a pot and then straining. So here is your very own 'mulled

Winter Spiced Jelly

jelly.' Spices were among the most demanded and expensive products available in Europe in the Middle Ages, the most common being black pepper, cinnamon, cumin, nutmeg, ginger and cloves – many of which have been used in this book. Given old medicinal theories of 'humorism', spices and herbs were indispensable to balance 'humors' in food, a daily basis for good health at a time of recurrent pandemics. Today, we know that many spices have anti-microbial and health-benefiting properties, but in these more prosperous times, spices are generally used as wonderful way to add variety and flavour to our dishes, so let's hope this jelly improves the 'humour' of your guests!

Winter Spiced Jelly

1kg Cooking Apples
400g Sugar
4 Leaves of Gelatine
100ml wine or cider vinegar
10 Cloves
7 Bay Leaves
4 Star Anise
4 Allspice Berries
2 Cinnamon Sticks
1 Teaspoon grated nutmeg
1 Orange / Lemon (for the peel)

Winter Spiced Jelly

1. Soften the gelatine in a bowl of water and chop the apples (including the core and peel) into chunks. **2.** Combine the apples, all the spices (save a few for decoration when the jelly is finished), peel and bay leaves into a heavy-bottomed saucepan. **3.** Pour over enough water to cover and bring to the boil. **4.** Then, turn down the heat and simmer with a lid or heavy plate on top for roughly one and a half hours. **5.** Pour the mixture into a jelly bag, and leave to strain overnight (remember not to squeeze it through yourself, as this will result in a cloudy jelly!) **6.** Once you have collected this liquid, pour it back into a heavy-bottomed saucepan, alongside the sugar and vinegar. **7.** Cook over a very low heat until everything is dissolved, stirring constantly. Once fully dissolved, boil for just over ten minutes. Then add the gelatine and stir over a lower heat. **8.** Now, test the setting point (see *Essential Skills*) and skim off any scum which may have risen to the surface. **9.** Pour your warm jelly into warm jars, and add any spices which may make an elegant garnish. Once the jelly has semi-set, you can push these into the middle, so they are not just floating on the top. **10.** Once your jelly is cold, it is ready to eat!

Herbal Highlights: Savoury Jellies

Jammy Judgements: Jellies

"The good setting of clear jelly seems to be a matter of greater pride than almost anything else in the kitchen and the more difficult a fruit is to jelly – such as strawberry or raspberry – the more boastful we become when we succeed.

Let my Grandmother have the last word. She always did in any case. 'When you make any kind of jelly take care you do not let any of the seeds from the fruit fall into your jelly, nor squeeze it too much, for that will prevent your jelly from being so clear. Pound your sugar and let it dissolve in the juice before you set it on fire, it makes the scum rise well and the jelly a better colour: it is a great fault to boil any kind of jellies too long, it makes them of a dark colour."

Ethelind Fearnon,
Jams, Jellies and Preserves – How to Make them *(1956)*

APPLE AND MINT JELLY

"The World is like a little marsh filled with mint and white hawthorn."

Mary Maclane

Mint has a very long history, and has been used for its digestion-aiding properties for centuries. It is thought that mint was introduced to Great Britain by the romans, and was referred to by a John Gardiner in his *Feate of Gardening* (1440) as 'myntys.' It was not until the early sixteenth century however, that mint was used for sauces (especially the traditional combination with lamb) in England. But after this date, it's been popular ever since! The smell of mint

Apple and Mint Jelly

is simply wonderful, as is its bright green colour, and it is just as good as a tea after dinner (just cut a few fresh leaves and pop them in a cup of boiling water). Mint in its various forms is really easy to grow at home, just make sure that you keep it in a pot as opposed to directly in the ground – as the roots do spread. So why don't you have a go at creating your own supply? Here is a lovely recipe for a mint and apple jelly, perfect as an unusual yet delicious addition to your traditional Sunday Roast.

Apple and Mint Jelly

1kg Cooking Apples

20g sprig of Fresh Mint

50g finely chopped Mint Leaves

500ml Water

200ml wine or cider vinegar

Caster Sugar (1g to 1ml of liquid produced)

Apple and Mint Jelly

1. Cut up the apples (cores and skins included) and place them in a heavy-bottomed saucepan. **2.** Add the sprig of mint and the water and simmer with the lid on until the apples are soft (this should take about thirty minutes.) **3.** Strain this mixture through a jelly bag over night, remembering not to squeeze it through if you would like a completely clear finished jelly. **4.** Put this juice and the vinegar back in a heavy-bottomed saucepan and heat on a low temperature. **5.** Then add the sugar (in a ratio of 1g to 1ml of liquid) and stir until completely dissolved. **6.** Bring the mixture to a rolling boil and after twenty minutes of cooking, test the setting point (see *Essential Skills*). **7.** If your jelly has reached its setting point, take it off the heat and stir in the remaining finely chopped mint. **8.** Leave the jelly to cool slightly and pour into warm, sterilised jars. Once it is sufficiently cold and set – your jelly is ready for consumption!

Basil Jelly

BASIL JELLY

Basil is one of the most widely used culinary herbs, and of course the main ingredient in pesto – an old Italian herb and oil sauce. Try this savoury jelly for an impressive addition to tomato salads (cut into thin slices with a little flaked sea salt for gourmet dining), as a meat marinade or even as a side to cream cheeses. Although originating in India, European uses of basil have been much debated; some thought it was good for the heart whilst others, such as Culpeper in the seventeenth century, linked it to poison. This was after he saw it help to draw venom from wounds – and followed the dictum 'like draws to like.' These conflicted meanings carried on into the Victorian era, when common basil signified hatred, but sweet basil was used to represent the giver's

Basil Jelly

best wishes. Whatever its folkloric origins though, people loved to eat this herb in a massive array of dishes. Basil is most commonly used fresh, so make sure not to cook it for too long otherwise this will completely ruin the wonderful strong flavours.

Basil Jelly

100g Basil
700ml Vegetable Stock
3 Gelatine Leaves

Basil Jelly

1. Pour the water into a saucepan and bring to the boil. **2.** Place the basil into the water for ten seconds (no more!) and immediately refresh it in iced water. **3.** Squeeze out any excess water and then blend the basil with the vegetable stock in a blender. **4.** Pass the mixture through a fine sieve, piece of muslin or jelly bag – making sure not to squeeze too much if you wish your jelly to be on the clearer side. **5.** Put the liquid back in the saucepan and bring to the boil. Then, lower the heat and add the gelatine and stir constantly until it is completely dissolved. **6.** Pour your basil jelly into containers (if you wish to create small squares – a shallow pan would work well, an ice-mould would be great for small cubes. **7.** Regular glass jars are just fine too). **8.** Once cool, your basil jelly is ready to eat.

Sage and Tarragon Jelly

In a very similar way to the apple and mint jelly, this sage and tarragon creation uses the natural pectin of the apples as a setting agent, with a little wine or cider vinegar added to bring up the 'tartness.' This ensures the jelly will be a lovely accompaniment to cold meats, tangy cheeses and as a glaze for roasts. Why not try melting some of this jelly over some mushrooms when you next cook them? Do, as with the mint, make sure to hold back some of the herbs, which you can stir through the jelly, once it has partially set. This will make a wonderful gift, as the freshly picked herbs suspended in the opaque jelly look thoroughly elegant. Tarragon is one of the four fines herbes of French cooking, also used for toothaches, digestion, aiding the heart and as an appetite stimulant.

Sage and Tarragon Jelly

Sage has a similarly long history, used since ancient times for warding off evil, snakebites, increasing women's fertility, and more. The Emperor Charlemagne recommended the plant for cultivation in the early Middle Ages and during the Carolingian Empire, it was cultivated in monastery gardens. In Britain sage has for generations been listed as one of the essential herbs, prized for its savoury, slightly peppery flavour along with parsley, rosemary and thyme (as in the folk song 'Scarborough Fair').

Sage and Tarragon Jelly

1kg Cooking Apples

1 large bunch of fresh sage

1 large bunch of fresh tarragon

700ml water

200ml wine or cider vinegar

Caster Sugar (1g to 1ml of liquid produced)

Sage and Tarragon Jelly

1. Cut up the apples (cores and skins included) and place them in a heavy-bottomed saucepan. **2.** Add the bunches of sage, tarragon (keep some small leaves behind for decoration) and the water. **3.** Simmer with the lid on until the apples are soft (this should take about thirty minutes.) **4.** Strain this mixture through a jelly bag over night, remembering not to squeeze it through if you would like a completely clear finished jelly. **5.** Put this juice and the vinegar back in a heavy-bottomed saucepan and heat on a low temperature. **6.** Then add the sugar (in a ratio of 1g to 1ml of liquid) and stir until completely dissolved. **7.** Bring the mixture to a rolling boil and after twenty minutes of cooking, test the setting point (see Essential Skills). **8.** If your jelly has reached its setting point, take it off the heat. **9.** Stir in the remaining small (or finely chopped) sage and tarragon leaves once the jelly is partially setting. **10.** Leave the jelly to cool slightly and pour into warm, sterilised jars. Once it is sufficiently cold and set – your jelly is ready for consumption!

WILD ROWAN JAM

"Any quantity of rowan berries and half their weight of sour apples, preferably the wild crab. Boil until soft and well mashed and drip through the jelly bag all night. Bring to the boil next day, add an equal quantity of sugar and boil very fast, about ten minutes."

The fruit of Rowan Berries has long been eaten in Britain, traditionally as an accompaniment to game (its pleasingly astringent taste goes very well with venison) and into jams and other preserves – on its own, or combined with other fruit. Rowans can also be used as a substitute for coffee beans, and have long been used to flavour liqueurs and cordials, to produce country wines and to flavour ale. British folklorists

Wild Rowan Jam

of the Victorian Era reported Rowan particularly useful for warding off witches, with Edwin Lees (1856) noting it being planted outside Midlands front doors, as did Sir James Frazer (1890) in Scotland. As it is most often found wild, on public land – rowan was a tasty but also cheap product to use in times of austerity; harsh yet sweet – a perfect combination! When you are picking your own berries, try to avoid the exceedingly bitter variants though, as these are not so good in jams.

Wild Rowan Jam

500g Rowan Berries
500g Cooking Apples
500g Sugar
1 Lemon

Wild Rowan Jam

1. Wash and take the stalks off the rowan berries.
2. Peel and cut the apples (cores and peel included).
3. But both the berries and the apples in a heavy-bottomed saucepan with enough water to cover.
4. Cook the fruits until the berries are soft (which should take about half an hour). **5.** Then, push the mixture through a sieve into a bowl. **6.** Place the sugar with a little water into a clean pot, heating until the sugar gets slightly brown (this will give your rowan jam a lovely, caramelised taste). **7.** Now, combine the rowan and apple with the sugar and cook this all together for a few minutes. **8.** Add a good squeeze of lemon. **9.** Test the setting point, and if your jam is ready (see *Essential Skills)* take it off the heat. **10.** Allow the jam to cool slightly, and then pour into warm, sterilised glass jars and seal.

English Herb Jelly

ENGLISH HERB JELLY

For Something a Little Different....
....Why not try, 'English Herb Jelly'?

Here, anything goes! The brilliant thing about making savoury herb jellies, is that you are in complete control of what you add into them. Once you have mastered the basic technique, you are in charge of the variations. Many herbs make great companions; rosemary and garlic with mint or parsley; fennel and marjoram with lemon thyme…or the aforementioned sage and tarragon. *How They Used To Do It* would have been simply to use whatever was most readily (and cheaply) available. You should be aiming for is a sweet yet piquant jelly though - so think about the herbs you would

English Herb Jelly

like to see as accompaniments to your regular dishes. We particularly recommend this version of a classically English herb jelly; a combination of lemon thyme, rosemary and a hint of garlic. It is a truly versatile jelly which can be used to add flavour to homemade stews, soups and gravies, giving a rich and rounded taste.

English Herb Jelly

1kg Cooking Apples
700ml Water
200ml wine or cider vinegar
A sprig of Lemon Thyme
A sprig of Rosemary
1 Large clove of Garlic
1 Lemon

English Herb Jelly

1. Cut up the apples (cores and skins included) and place them in a heavy-bottomed saucepan. **2.** Add the bunches of thyme and rosemary (keeping some small leaves behind for decoration), the chopped garlic (here, feel free to add more or less according to taste) and the water. **3.** Simmer with the lid on until the apples are soft (this should take about thirty minutes.) **4.** Strain this mixture through a jelly bag over night, remembering not to squeeze it through if you would like a completely clear finished jelly. **5.** Put this juice and the vinegar back in a heavy-bottomed saucepan and heat on a low temperature. **6.** Then add the sugar (in a ratio of 1g to 1ml of liquid) and stir until completely dissolved. **7.** Bring the mixture to a rolling boil, add a good squeeze of lemon and after twenty minutes of cooking, test the setting point (see Essential Skills). **8.** If your jelly has reached its setting point, take it off the heat. **9.** Stir in the remaining small (or finely chopped) thyme and rosemary leaves once the jelly is partially setting. **10** Leave the jelly to cool slightly and pour into warm, sterilised jars. Once it is sufficiently cold and set – your jelly is ready for consumption!

Serving Suggestions

Serving Suggestions

There are so many ways to serve jams and jellies, and hopefully we have given you some ideas with each recipe. The great thing about jams and jellies, is that they can be paired with savoury or sweet foods alike - think quince with cheese, blackberries with pork (instead of the standard apple sauce), cranberry with stuffing, raspberry with chocolate, elderflower with rhubarb and roses with delicate desserts.

The list goes on. Try to think of the fruit or flavouring on its own, and what foods you would pair that with normally – and then exactly the same will apply to your jam or jelly! For the beginners, try experimenting by using a new flavour in a tried and tested recipe. Half the fun is in the trialling, so be brave…

Serving Suggestions

Serving Suggestions

BRAVE ENOUGH FOR THESE?

Here are some serving suggestions from the 1950s, some do sound better than others.

"Try for instance…

Plum-Walnut-and-raisin jam or fig-and-carrot with curry.

Lime-and-pineapple with duck.

Marmalade with apple pie, bacon or kippers.

Green gooseberry fool with mackerel.

Rose-petal jam with yoghurt.

Serving Suggestions

Parsley jelly with boiled cod or poultry.

Spiced blackberry jelly with grilled cod.

Mint jelly with cold lamb.

Damson cheese with hot boiled ham.

Rose-hip jelly with jugged hare.

Rowan or apple jelly with rabbit or pork.

Crab apple jelly with venison.

And your household will never complain of the dullness of meals again."

(We're pretty sure of that!)

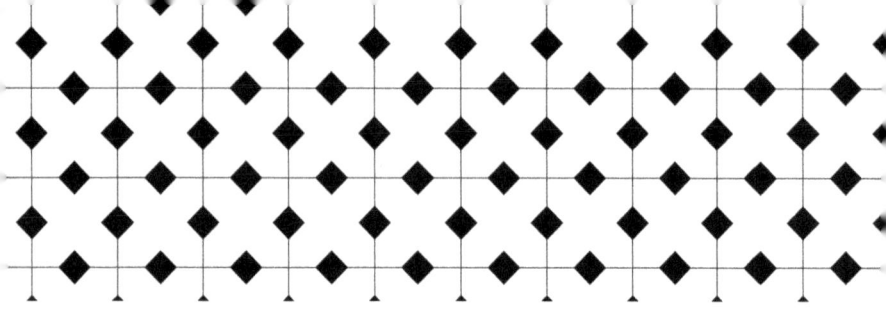

Gorgeous Gifts

Gorgeous Gifts

As we said in the introduction to this little book, the wonderful thing about making your own homemade products is the fun one can have with creating customised labels and garnishes to the finished jars (think berries, citrus zest, herb sprigs). For the flower jams and jellies, a few fresh flowers are beautiful accompaniments - either inside the clearer jellies or scattered on top. Exactly the same applies for the berries, fruits and spices; whatever main ingredient you have used, save some back for decoration afterwards. Jams and Jellies really do make the perfect vintage-inspired present as well as personal treat.

Make sure to source some lovely glass jars (kilner 'clip tops' work well, as do the traditional jam jar which you will find

Gorgeous Gifts

in most homeware stores). This will instantly make your creations look the part. As well as this, for serving jellies at dinner parties, there are so many wonderfully decorated and inventive moulds out there, so have a bit of fun! At this point, you can also make your own tags (think brown card and twine) to hang around the top of the jars, as well as handwritten labels to adorn the your containers. You could also place a little square of material ('gingham' is always lovely, though 'paisley' would also look a treat) over the top of your jar. Tied with some twine, this gives a great vintage-inspired twist to your presents, and we're sure the recipients will be touched by your efforts. Good luck, and happy decorating.

Ten Top Tricks and Tips

1. Fruit should *always* be sound, ripe (or really, slightly under), but never *over-ripe* – clean and dry. Fruit picked in wet (or even continuously foggy weather) makes jam and jellies which will develop mould in a very short time.

2. For jams in general, fruit should be boiled gently until cooked - *before* the sugar is added, then boiled *fast* for a *short* time until it jells. The flavour will be more like fresh fruit if this method is followed. But if it is over-boiled *after* adding sugar, the flavour, colour and consistency will all suffer.

3. Always stir well until the sugar is dissolved! Additionally, a wooden spoon is best for *stirring* and a metal one to remove scum as it gathers.

4. Do not use *too* large quantities of fruit at a time – large quantities are extremely difficult to handle without the proper equipment.

5. A pinch of bicarbonate of soda, added to very sour fruits (such as lemon or gooseberry) counteracts the acid, and less sugar is required.

Ten Top Tricks and Tips

6. Always have jars warm, ready for your jams and jellies.

7. The only exception to this above rule for jams is berried fruits – leave these until cool before putting into jars. This prevents berries from rising.

8. A great way to test the set of your jams and jellies is to put some on a cold plate – and when it has cooled, hold the plate vertical. If the jam remains on the plate it is cooked. If its on the floor – it isn't! This applies equally to jellies.

9. Store in a dry, cool place. The greatest enemies to jams and jellies are mould and crystallization. As long as they do not encounter any steam or heat after production, your products should keep for a very long time.

10. Do make sure your jars are properly sterilised, as the cleanliness of equipment is probably one of the most important factors in the shelf-life of your home-made jams and jellies.

But most importantly, just have fun!

Credits and Attributions

Cover Image, Title page and Page 4 - This work is a derivative of "1956-Electrolux" is copyright © October 17, 2009 James Vaughn, x-ray delta one, made available on Flickr under Creative Commons Attribution 2.0 Generic (CC BY 2.0) http://www.flickr.com/photos/x-ray_delta_ one/4017899831/sizes/l/in/faves-90808113@N04/

Page 28 - This work is a derivative of "It's All You Need" is Copyright © 1950 Posted by noluck_ boston, made available on vintage-ads.livejournal.com http://vintage-ads.livejournal.com/tag/cleaning

Page 34 - This work is a derivative of "LIFE Dec 12, 1955 hamilton watches christmas spread" is Copyright © 1955, posted by Jocelmeow, made available on vintage-ads.livejournal.com http://vintage-ads.livejournal.com/tag/1945

Page 37 - This work is a derivative of "Maxwell House Coffee (1950) " is Copyright © 1950 posted by, pikkewyntjie made available on vintage-ads.livejournal.com http://vintage-ads.livejournal. com/tag/1950

Page 178 - This work is a derivative of "Tiffany Blue" is Copyright © May 18, 2008, Jill Clardy, made available on flickr under Creative commons Attribution 2.0 Generic (CC BY 2.0) http://www.flickr.com/photos/jillclardy/2523850043/

Page 179 - This work is a derivative of "UH-OH - Oreo / Nabisco, 1951" is Copyright © 1951, posted by Man Writing Slash (write_light), made available on vintage-ads.livejournal.com http://vintage-ads.livejournal.com/tag/1919